# WAVES OF GRACE

**Anna Grace**

First Published February 2017
© 2017

All rights reserved. No part of this book may be copied or distributed in any other binding without written permission from the publisher. It may, however, be fairly quoted for the purpose of review.

ISBN: 978-1-7345704-6-5

# Contents

| | |
|---|---|
| Choosing you Part 1 | 1 |
| Choosing you part 2 | 7 |
| Blank | 12 |
| Africa | 13 |
| Soul | 16 |
| Earth | 17 |
| Magpie | 18 |
| Hers | 24 |
| Drive | 26 |
| Minute | 30 |
| Wind | 32 |
| Ruby | 33 |
| Lunar | 34 |
| Life | 36 |
| Fly | 37 |
| Story | 38 |
| John Wayne | 40 |
| Mag | 43 |
| Skies | 44 |
| Love | 45 |
| Craig's | 46 |

| | |
|---|---|
| Found | 50 |
| Friday | 51 |
| Jenn | 56 |
| Timothy | 58 |
| Blue | 60 |
| Braille | 61 |
| Nirvana | 62 |
| Gods | 63 |
| Moved | 64 |
| Stay | 67 |
| Lullaby | 69 |
| Light's | 71 |
| Jordan | 72 |
| Name | 73 |
| That | 74 |
| Tattoo | 75 |
| Snap | 76 |
| In | 77 |
| White | 78 |
| Fine | 80 |
| Faith | 88 |
| Feb | 89 |
| Daniel | 90 |
| Rain | 92 |
| Dream | 94 |
| God | 95 |
| Humanity | 96 |

| | |
|---|---|
| Stars | 99 |
| Tangent | 100 |
| Full Moon Dreaming | 103 |
| Bardot | 111 |
| Dogs | 112 |
| Mess | 114 |
| Delusions | 116 |
| Tear Drops | 118 |
| Sydney strangers | 121 |
| All | 128 |
| Breathe | 131 |
| Cave | 133 |
| Cars | 134 |
| You | 138 |
| Thee | 140 |
| Memory | 142 |
| Katie | 147 |
| Nineteen | 149 |
| Pack | 155 |
| Time | 156 |
| Shacks | 157 |
| Hurt | 158 |
| Nothing | 159 |
| Boy | 160 |
| Him | 161 |
| Blue | 163 |
| Fly | 164 |

# Choosing you Part 1

It was rehearsed in my mind
To write some of this
Echoes of a past I reclaim as my own
Yet there is no way to do justice
To so called illness, experience, choice or circumstance
At its height
I was a conveyor belt,
A Nazi,
Slave to a disease ravaging my existence
I witness fear
In other's eyes
Like deer hearts,
Running for cover
Not my own Though
I'd go flying
I'd lay on my mother's bed,
Reserved for queens, Reading and dreaming
Of banana bread, and being sleek barefoot
Playing the piano
It was a long time ago, yet like the grief
Of losing a loved one,
It never ever
Really truly
Goes away

You just learn to deal with it
Perfectionism can be an imprint
A DNA
And common for the falling.
The striving
Theescapists
You don't chooseit
It choosesyou
I can recall my defining moment. That was it. I was to get super fit, lean, free, empty, the best I could be.
A private Ali. "I am the greatest."
I'd run for miles
In the fog. Dirt road beginnings
And I was Hitler about it
Discipline
My greatest ally and friend
It's what we do.
What an addict does.
No room for slip-ups
In disease,
Is there?
You see, I was gaining control over my body
The only thing that belonged to 'me'
Was completely 'mine'
And could not be dictated by 'them'...
In some respect I was actually Losing control
Of worldly, accepted, societal existence
You get empty. Heavy. Light. Cold. Freezing. Ravaged in darkness.

Your own
And Everyone's
The hurt
Of the entire World can be felt.
In your skeletal structure
Is that it?
We want to stop feeling?
Oh love,
There are no quick fixes
No vaccinations
For sensitives
You get it
Or youdon't
Feel it all. Or feel nothing.
Go for all
At least you can exit battered and bruised.
Well lived
At your finish line
Tasting many apples
Bitter Sweet Melodies
So there you go fall
And then you dig yourself
Out again
And again
Scrambling to the light.
Sometimes with help
From animals
Or others
Mainly spirit

My introduction to darkness
Mine.
My daddy's,
And mine.
You can't pinpoint or point blame.
Everyone had their theories
Poor little rich girl
Which I can say are bullshit. Bullshit.
They are just theories to tick the box, encourage parents
to believe they didn't completely fuck up.
In my mind, mine did quite a bit, a lot.
At the time
I never wanted money
Or worldly possessions
I wanted simple.
Love, affection, hugs. Easy.
Normal.
Nothing more. Appreciation.
Free to be me.
A birthright.
Everyone's
Until I took it away from myself,
Almost,
And even unjustly blamed them...
They did their best
They did all they could do All they knew how
They didn't know
You could change. Break cycles
I always had

An element of wild
I needed permission to fly
A chance
Not an intellect I often became
In a box.
Bereft
Of heart
And soul.
That isn't who I am, who I was....
No soft edges
I needed soft edges
Room to move
Apparent success is a crock of shit. Surface moulding
I was o.k. Smart.
Achieving, God I hate that word.
Keeping it together.
It is a cover up
The barest of souls Float the finest Bite the hardest and
chew only in the gaps
They are able
A journey
Of beginnings and ends, my sacred contract
Weakness isn't sickness and Sickness is not weakness
Yet my greatest strengths
Turned out
And still do
To be my greatest weakness
Baring of soul is scary
To onlookers

Who prefer to hide gossip behind comfort cars and glory
And peer down misty glasses muttering
Thank god, it's not them
If only they knew
That it actually is....
He looked after troubled young teens
Boasted no deaths bed programs
To save lives
I didn't go there. But met many who did Nasogastric
tubes Teddies by their side Concerned boyfriends,
If they chose to stick around that far.
And one girl
Left us
And it rocked him
The doc
A lot
She lost her dog
The last straw. Whenfur
And its love Is the only thing
Keeping
Your feet on the floor
I get it.
To be cont...

# Choosing you part 2

Day of nothings another day in
wilderness,
secret enchantments, forgotten nights you
tell her, she hears them say
no, no you tell her
they stop, startled as she enters the room hates it
when they do that
smokescreens, like videogames
cover-ups for whatever it is they
can't handle
visible woundings
it is different if you look good they
want you when they want you
when money, fame, fortune, possessions poor
little rich girls do not fit
tattoos, piercings, skinfolds and stretchmarks
enough to repulse your mother
oh, for fuck sake just come out and say it you
are going to die too

Spectacular falls from grace
hiding from what, from whom, for whom?
her brother is a god
like James Hird, Leonardo Dicaprio, Rob Lowe or

somebody like that
his eyes, green and blue, perfectly round
chin a dimple
perfect in the middle sensitivity has, but
then overtly lacks
when it comes to things of depth
things that matter
he never bloody speaks, except when drunk she
wants to shake him
"Show something, anything!" but
it's her stuff
ostrich in the sand
Aquarian mind fit for bears and footballers lusts
for breasty women
to be held by his lovers
rocked to sleep at night
like all those nights he bashed his head on the wall she
wonders why he did that?
did he torment him too? she
couldn't share his room he
would say nothing
blink his big eyes
he is adorable though
you'd want to melt in his arms
there's just something about the guy, he's yummy and he
knows it
twenty-six, could no longer get out of bed swollen
glands, adrenals shot
something was up, nobody believed her
proof, a name, a box, something

mum said, I don't think you want to finish this bloody
university degree
oh god, if only she knew my lust for the piece of paper vomit
always in the mornings orange
juice and cashew nuts air was
horrifying
short to come by
blood tests biopsies, time wasting valuable
valuable time
eleven doctors, scars, stitches
beginning of the end
the end of the road sporting
career, academia lovers, on
backburners dreams sent to
clouds
naturopath
don't give up
greens, blues and purples
you've got it
the madonnas
I would go and sit in intensive care
Sue smoked like a train, an Elizabeth Taylor,
a Marilyn Monroe
she may die
I would go in and stroke her hand and pray
nobody knew
I would massage her fingers and send her
blessings her husband was in tears
it was the first time I saw David cry it
just wasn't her time

you are not in charge of this holy place you
you just ride her
English teacher, like robin williams so
delicious, she could eat him
full of spunk, intellect and interesting experience
English master yet had no formal education rigged
the system love it
something exciting about that
it's a turn on
they had something he
loved her
soft spots up for the taking, seldom delivered
delicacies of extended family
oh damn, isn't it ironic, the time the place the age
always something
until you jump off
the cliff
and never stop falling
madonnas, buddhas blue, butterflies black and orange you
came out crying, gasping for breath
do you remember?
the tenderness of your mother's nipple
her teardrop on your bloodied head so
special
so, so special
such a relief
you won't go out the same way
though waterfalls
whisper
oceans break

birds fly
stay
as soon enough
they
will be choosing you too

*~Blank~*

And A
Blank
Canvas Is
So Sexy

# ~Africa~

Please don't bellow Nobody will
hear your screams.
Nor cry wolf
We get sick of the same old stories.
Purple stars and orange hearts
you've been it all before.
Don't wait till he's gone to
tell him you love him or
ache to smell his skin touch
his shoulders
or hear his dream One
more time.
Nor wait to give him that
picture you painted of him
on the bridge
as hamlet.
He sleeps shirt off
socks on
eyelashes like a four year old's.
Divine Orbs encircle him.
Don't even lock the doors anymore they're
already open
Known to those who care.
And the faeries you saw in the garden tell

your heart they were real
They probably were.
Stories of astrology that most
don't believe in
go to the stars from here to Arizona and
ask the one that falls shiny blue closest
to you into your lap
what it really means.
And Elliot the butterfly presence of quiet
sage like characters
quivering in your sacred places they
are all around
Long before you came and I went and
I came and you went.
Ashes and stardust
heavens and creations
you hold her in your own bare hands.
When not easy to love and
hard to handle
the gentlest gods are needed. We
ride in similar spheres you and I
The same
even.
One body You
belong here.
There will always be greater and lesser than
Yourself
With tyranny there always is.
A beautiful sister who was
once afraid of

dark

upon hearing an afrikan woman speak post
escaping slums
rape and various atrocities said "walk
forwards.
Always Walk forwards into
the danger....
and melt all away "

# ~Soul~

Why do you do it, sell your soul like that? Where
does it get you anyway? he asked.
She shrugs,
eyes blue, lines
drawn,
frown line more evident.
The moon was full.
The stars were dancing, The
comets alive.
Well, she said, if it helps another it's
worth it.
Without soul food You are
fucking dead alive. He shrugs,
holds her hand
And they walk....
to the ocean...

# ~Earth~

I like a man who can cry in front of me. And
rest his dragon wings in my lap.
I like the sound of a grown man weeping, like
somehow a new earth is being born.

# ~Magpie~

It rained the day you went away.
Pearly blue greys and trees that dance like
1950's women.
Elegant like wildfires.
Pushing the needle too far.
You me her. Exquisite.
I like that word. it
does things.
Let go I said
he struggles for breath.
It is ok.
Don't be afraid.
Last earthly oxygen. what
else to say to death?
My buddha man.
My papa.
Surly grin stouts firm hands ties a delight.
Pink carnation in hand. His
soul would not leave while
Mum was around.
Souls.
They Do that.
Woke 5am.
Knew . he'd

gone.
think of him daily.
Almost.
Then I fell in love. As I tend to do.
Only a fool pities the fool.
Until a crash
A softening a ball of crumpled ash.
I fell in love with a feeling.
With her. it.
I did.
Mary Magdalene hands on feet.
Took the trip.
held
god's hands
motherland.
Liver anguish anchored in body.
I let go.
I just .... let go.
Left.
You
are going to be a phenomenal healer one day
she said.
hair thin eyes large piercing blue
behind glasses
dimpled smile erect spine a
lefty. Kind. Gentle.
Virgo wings visible she
got me.
the creek 26 tears
A death a new beginning. best

friend in dangerous place.
the year I took him camping for his birthday. warm
fire country pub rugged up regal. burgundy cords
black top
slim fit cross Legged
Sexed up.
lay back on couch.
him, just him. fire.
perfect. irreverent
times. Pockets of
magic.
don't take that. for granted.
Ever.
Creek a swag.
sparkling burgundys
To soften edges. thrill
chase embrace unions
candles smashing in the snow
crisp naked with socks on. me on
top hair tickling his chest
way he liked it.
Me holding his jaw, both hands.
The kiss. way I liked it.
Pockets of magic.
Do you still think of me?
I miss our bubble.
highway hummers pushing to limits. tell me
do you still think of me?
then her.
A brush of breast shoulders white

thin shirt.
tingles like wildfire.
Kundalini,
something alive.
waist held squeezes past.
Be careful. Be so very careful.
Unspeakable understandings. Only
her, could open me like that. just
hands on feet.
she got me.
Her soul on
mine.
Illusion or delusion.
Folk fall in love with me too you know.
Yet
it was not me.
But my
touch.
Essence.
vortex.
Themselves, us. She
controlled him.
the gardener, she could.
tall poppies and blood red roses
entwirl her room.
African animals line the wall. really
he ruled her. Her longing.
I wanted to hug her. save her
from what?
Solace in books overwork her garden moon

animals and healing.
the world and
children.
her touch so kind and generous. like a
natalie merchant
or sarah mclachlan song. her
soul sang melodies
when embraced in her presence.
others found her distant.
I found her cool.
Clear uncomplicated.
hands on feet sent me flying or crying. one
or the other.
I deserved this. Feeling rhythm instantly.
My prize. my angel
Motherly calm Mentor.
nurtured when close.
tuned in from afar.
Thank you woman. Thank you
she would retreat to her cave in the snow.
Like pema
words do not explain energy.
Katie said you have this thing, hooks, of
making everyone feel at ease
With themselves. Nice. give
what crave. overflowing then.
takes shit for that point.
Connected,
healing. Feeling eyes Seeing hands, mystery
excitement unknown.

I write for what.
Whom Why
Now?
live. and die each day. Is it
a full moon again?
to the educateds sensitives wizards crazies
magicians and sages.
trust in unfolding of magics.
The mysteries.
Her agenda. The
magic and You.

# ~ Hers ~

She looked more fragile than she should Far thinner
And lines I'd never seen before
Sunken yet still elegant Sturdiness of woman
shimmering through
She does this sometimes.
I know when something has her.
Time alone is so rare, I value it
Momentary understandings Potent
like our Piscean moon We are,
As Trust leaks in.
We do have this thing, beyond the crap.
Where we feel like friends, again.
She is kind yet blind, driven by another, Not
her own.
But the bitter castle
With bamboo jars are still up for the taking,
Bitterness scorns in the end eats gall bladders And
crowds like grey your lungs.
She is her father's heart, thank god, but a little less lady And
some real broken could heal the purges.

Necessary, or are they?
I love her wildly. Beyond skin.
Beyond measure and recognition

The little mermaid girl in me loves her with my entirety:
Despite injustices, ill grievances yet explained.
We both crave gentle, the indigenous and childlike.
A time that's coming...a time That
is...surely coming...
Soon... God
I love her...

# ~Drive~

Don't leave it below the surface It
breathes
' Truth '
Like a butterfly in bloom Dolphins
frolicking
They made love in her bedroom The
room was hot
Fan churning He
breathes her
Fleshed and knighted Nails
claw his back Hair tickles
his nipples She fingers his
navel And earlobes
And tongues his stomach The
last protruding bit God, he
whispered
God I fucking love you She
knows this
But struggles to love him back Coz
of the what ifs
What if there is better out there

What if she wants to sail alone
What if he reads her dark side?

What if he takes all of her?
The better parts?
They climbed the waterfall To
the top
He stood there Gazing into the
never never
Like already lost She feared
he may jump
Love does that Pushes
you to jump
And his disclaimer, nobody gets him Except her
Which can be a tight glove if mishandled They
were getting it
Like the tides Oceans
The runaways
Getaways Come
closers
It didn't happen They
got torn apart
Lines down the middle

Charity over comfort
He fell in love with her free spirit Her
wild endeavour
She fell in love with his depth, His
rock like character
His dimple and jaw And
his fingers
That could play her like a piano
Nobody

Nobody else got her like that
Sanskrit, unspoken
Love loved Then lost
She heard screams from the balcony Then
saw herself
From above, screaming Yet no
sound came out
Ike the night a man grabbed her from behind
Some sicko getting his thrills
She screamed
Not much sound came out
Then kneed him in the groin and ran like hell No
neighbours came out
Nobody

This deflated her She
got away
She saw the birth of Evan By
caesarean section Carefully
attuned and timed What an
honour
His first cry, his bloodied head Dark hair
and scrunched perfect face
A new life A
presence
Entering our planes You
were born free, silly
Unskinned
Before ordered chaos
Skin off

Will happen
Otherwise life
Rides you Ride
Ride Ride Baby
We, drive tonight

# ~Minute~

Do You
Ever have those moments
Where you just break down Coz
something
Is almost too beautiful to touch To be
true
Or almost too painful to feel
And it may not even be Yours
Do you ever have those moments?
Of complete oneness
In the presence of no human company Or
there is too much passion
To keep your feet on the floor
A cosmic explosion of love And
intellectual expression Of art
and funky and colour Or you skip
boundlessly
For no fucking reason Even
when things are dark And
tragic
Like a butterfly in the rain

Yet feeling Makes all
possible

Keep on giving
Keep on giving
Keep on Giving
One more...
Time Otherwise
Just otherwise
Those magic minutes
Hours, seconds
Yep Those...
How fragile
We are...

# ~Wind~

Frozen
Like that night at Lake Tahoe The
Aztecs
Singing their ceremony The light
shattering the wind The breeze
blowing your name
Frozen
When you don't know what to do You
just want a bed
By the fire or under the sun
You want your dog Niggling
your ear
And you realise
Again
And again
This absurd nonsense of attachment
Is like
A candle In
the Wind

# ~Ruby~

He undressed her With
his mind...

# ~ *Lunar* ~

The world just got a little quieter
It was the last day of December A
beautiful dawn
Amber rains They'd been
for a surf
Crystal clear yet freezing Seals
sat by and the sun set Finally
They emerged from the water
Brewed tea by the van And
warmed by a fire
" I dreamt of Bali last night" she said
" and kali, Buddha and a party on the beach And
yoga, and surfing the impossible "
"cool" he smiles
"and I dreamt you died, Got
sucked out by the swell "
He paused, frowned then leant in to kiss her His
whiskers tickle her cheeks
His angelic frame, edible eyes
excruciatingly clear
His heart, impeccable, like his word
Almost too good to be true Really
They laugh as friends,
family, earth maidens And

lovers
She fears losing him In
those quiet moments when
the thunder rises
And the air is still
And things seem a little easy Like laying
in on a Sunday morning
She fears losing him To the
ocean, the moon
nature's perils To
another lover
Or even his mother
She likes Fooling with thunder
Everyone whispers
Their love is enough though He is enough
You are enough With
Or without Him....

Life
All about
How you deal
With plan B.

# ~ Fly ~

Some souls transverse a while
then they are gone

# ~Story~

Tell me your story That I
may be so wise As to say
nothing

Show me you're broken
That I may be so brave As to
be broken too

Show me your loneliness
fuckups
desires and intuitions That I may
be vulnerable too

Show me your human side
addictions, greed
feathers and disposition Your
openness
sexiness and
fears
Stand at the cliff of disbelief
And Shout to the rooftops Of
wanting more

Kiss me
Even when he's looking And
drink me, alive
I'll stand by you
And trust
You'll stand by me too

As I meet you, again
On the far side In
the middle

I love you

# ~ John Wayne ~

I want to know
Why how if Will
you?
I want to know Why
You are driven by the need to
understand
Me
Why you stand above yourself In
dark hours
Hallucinogenic memoirs  Looking
down upon the gravesite Ridden with
red roses
And angels for stardust
Atoms as your eyes Stencils
in your veins Why you
watch him tattooed and
ugly eyed
Filled to the brim with ethanol
Scars on wrists Daggers in veins
Yet his heart walks miles

To be with you And him
He smiles and hugs you down

by the river
cooks you dinner catches you fish tells
you this is not his homeland He's a
Blackman
And you get to call him By
his Blackman name As he
invited you in
The moment you touched down as
you gained insight
to his condition
He considers you Blackman Too
What a privilege
This life
rivers of mercy
new beginnings
In the dawn of dawn His brother
his son his uncle His kidney
doing backflips
I might be mad, he says He is not

There is nothing wrong with him
A series of hardships blinds wary soul He
went to the grave of his mother Wept
waterfalls
For hours Whispering
her name Carrying her
spirit Like bats for lashes
We are the ancestors
Channels

The whispers
The brave left to battle Together
Again.

# ~Mag~

Don't tell grief to get over it People
are irreplaceable
Certain souls
turn you inside out
With their
Magic...

# ~Skies~

She may never know How
many tears I cried
For her little boy just born Named
and left after
Five days
She may never know I cursed the gods and
Angels on her behalf
For sending him away
She may never know I feel her Tiny frame And
vulnerability inside my own
Her heart bleeds like a ghost
As her mother flies high in the skies
Whispering
Her name


(I love you C.P )

# ~Love~

If I loved you for a moment I
loved you for a lifetime
If I drank your smile And felt
your hollowness
Beneath mine
should I wonder what you her
or I, are here for
I will spread myself thin, Just
to Get to you
As this
Is
No Ordinary Love

# ~Craig's~

She strode corridors
of lonely ghosts fallen
angels
skins in waiting dolls
of the underground.
I held her hand massaged
her fingers listened to her
smile her words
on Jesus and
god
whatever that means her
time is here
it is coming and she
knows it she has died
before
yet to claim it
sent energy through the elbow
heart and veins
bent her leg motionless
yet warm
she clenched her fist
and worked from her shoulder
smile
and sighs the

both of us
two's become one
"I either want to
get well
or just go in my
sleep..."
hope
a distant friend at times stroke
claiming her muscles and
control
" I will see my mother again, what
happens
is I go underground and
wait for Jesus " she said
" then I go to god "
whatever, I thought.
Ambivalent no
judgement music
streamed
from across the
corridor irritating
gnarlish
I walked to the room and asked if
I could turn it down He obliged and
with a dribble said sure
I waited, as Alanis came
on my nemesis
so I watched and imagined
being her.
I am her.

actually...
His name was Craig and
he was divine is divine
barely audible
and with a dribble I held his hand fuck
I thought
fuck, this poor beautiful man this
beautiful beautiful man
I asked how long he is in here,
the hospital. "forever" he mumbled
shit, I thought
when I asked of his condition
he pointed to his alphabet but I could not get it.
Parkinson's?
Cerebral palsy? "
no..."
it didn't matter.
We were connecting
this beautiful beautiful
tragic man
who was confined to chair, could
no longer speak
feed himself nor
walk,
yet he was so polite.
And warm.
I am in love
right now so
thankful.
I just held his hand in

silence
then conversed.
Stroked his hand and leg His
dull eyes shone a little He has
a daughter
13 years  old He has a
heartbeat
He has a fucking heartbeat, and I
held his hand
That
Was
Enough...Thank you

# ~Found~

They found each other
They were always Going to find one another
The gods orchestrated the dance
When
they were no longer
Looking

# ~ Friday ~

This is for you
For us
For you
For the law of least efforts
For living and dying
For you
and all the times you put him
ahead of your needs, your
mother's grief
before your own, your
wanting to fail
as the finish line is just Too
bloody close.

This is for you
when you want to give up.
But dancing together
makes you hold on one
more day.

This is for you
when needles and injections Aren't
enough to cure a flailing heart.

## Waves of Grace

This is for you when
looking cool
Was more important than prosperity,
image more important than authenticity,
when you lied
To save another's arse to save
grace for someone
who didn't actually give a fuck.
Again.

This is for you
whose hormones ate you alive.
For giving him away despite him
wanting you And you, him
A Shakespearean tragedy Sliding
doors of heaven and hell As
friendship is more dear
than honest breaking hearts.

This is for you who is
judged for being
sleep deprived, childless and motionless
and random,
but oh so beautiful
So excruciatingly beautiful
Time and again.

This is for you,
insensitive yet numb
You who crawls through open ghosts And

fucks the earth
with reckless abandon.

This is for you
Who could murder your father
The night you went black and unchecked.

This is for you the
wannabe artist
We are all artists you know The
magician who knows stuff
From sages and ages most would
not even contemplate to admit

This is for you Matt
drives to the coast, our tears and ecstasy
Lotus straddles on my bed
surfing on Malibu's and that late night walk The
scenic under the stars.
When we remembered.
And I realised you were, are, one of us.
I got you baby. I
really did.
God.

This is for you
unafraid of emotions
Keeping in check your devotion
To love and life and love and life and love....

This is for you Who
chose to stay Chooses
to stay Despite it all
When you could have gone
And for those who went
Well...

This is for you
Who may feel the pain of the world Yet
dive in anyway
Isn't it just amazing
Is there any other way really?

This is for you
with the twinkle blue eyes
Snippets of magic
Oh god I want to touch you
The heart flutters that keep me alive Daily
Hourly

This is for you
who danced with devils
And underground lovers amidst fairy
dust foraging for truth

This is for you
A rain check of promises the
I'll be there
when you are clearly absent
again.

This is for you
who chooses
Tenderness over selfish gain
middle ground over ecstasy Our
shades of confusion Dissolved

This is for you Who
came out alive
Somehow,
Somehow

This is for you And the
middle man
You are still the middle man.
My middleman.
And if I forget to tell you I
never
Ever
stopped
Loving You

## ~ Jenn ~

She's a wildfire
Dandelion in spring Eye
for justice
All things beautiful Her
restless heart Rips
For new beginnings Seduced by
dangerous liaisons
In days gone by With
the older man Naively
confident
A Princess of Babylon
Black widow to angels
Don't fuck
with her compassion though It
cuts like a sword
She makes love with edges God knows
she's been plenty before
She dances with erotic poetry,
Fairy tales and truth
Can be flower girl, or Madonna And
make love on a train,
cross-country, all in the same
day She'd hit your ex
If your life depended on it And

she'd give you her sweater
In five degree rains
Seeker for truth
An eye for exquisite And
rebellion
Cerebrum for diplomacy Body
for pleasure
And heart
Not bereft of courage
She finds a wave And
will ride it
To the end She
has a way
Weed may tame monkey minds Or
when the world
Gets too much But her
lust for life Sensual
pleasure
And expression To
touch
Will captivate your soul

Too.
Thank you Jennifer

# ~Timothy~

And
Do you still think of me Like I
do you?
I move forward carelessly
Restlessly
Yet
I would be the woman
Who holds your face In
the very hands
that caressed you The
first time
To let you know it was ok Is ok
To cry in my lap When you
lost someone
Your supposed Forever
there
I want to know what keeps
you awake at night What
makes you tick What makes
you alive What burns your
feathers
And what pisses you
off And do you do
darkest hours?

And do you want
my waist
Face Or
mind The
most
I want to kiss away your tears And
you mine
Wiping and placing your lips On my
cheeks dancing
With gold
The stuff dreams are made of
And as we rest at night And
drink the moon
Your hand reaches to my breast And
casually asks if it's my shoulder As we
drift to another plane together
As if we died that night As if
we died
We died
And if I had not met you
Surely
I would
have dreamed you
Into existence You
Beautiful
You...
Beautiful...

## ~Blue~

Boys posing as
men Fast cars
Sunset boulevards
Child smiles Dog
whispers Moon
beams
And I
Still
Miss you madly

# ~Braille~

Darling
Be my braille
should I
answer,
To you...

# ~Nirvana~

Embodied wisdom
Caves in the snow

# ~Gods~

Gods as monsters
Love
As no mistake....

## ~Moved~

I want to be moved
I want to cry at your sheer sight I
want to fall
bare chest crucifix
driven straight
through

I want to be moved
whether joy
grief belittled
or anguish
Of the ecstasy you cried seeing
her birthed
this life
sweet angel of yours
mine
ours in
time.

I want to be moved by
the simple
the stifled the
black dog
and the ignorant
sheathed and pretty.

I want to be moved
seeing you sigh
as I caress your thigh
stroke your hips
and touch your frown lines that
make me cry.
I want to be moved
knowing you love me like
your first
your forever
your always.

I want to be moved thinking
of my mother and her
wannabe lovers falling at
her feet
her naivety her
grief
of what is forgotten.

I want to be moved
As I orgasm
to your heart's belonging as
you squirm and shudder like a
quake eternal
the rock
exploding
from beneath the tombs
The embers.

I want to be moved knowing
your haughtiness comes from
my depth mermaid like
tentacle confused
clear candescent and
not my breasts.

I want to be moved
seeing the cloud
rainforests sunlight and
grains the aboriginal
dirty drunken with spirit Whiteman
cannot even fathom spirit deep
in his eyes
I cry with ecstasy truly
I do.

I want to be moved carrying you with
me him with me too
I want to be moved like a
baby puppy hurled
fallen at your feet near
the open fire blazing
echoing your name.
I
just
want
to be moved.

(this is so much easier. if you are with me.)

# ~Stay~

A splash a flash a dolphin A
moment in disguise
A spleen severed Sits
on the sidewalk can do
without it
her happy submerged underwater
Organic. Light. Feminine. Raw.
Wild men wear halos
long beards
tanned shoulders reeking
of sex driving mad
her a haiku flower she aches she
burns yet returns for more of what?
She misses her dog in
this realm exquisitely
so especially now and
the bearded brown
eyed man
with the lashes
who conquered
unheard parts of her
unknown to herself
aching to be shed unseen
yet together

left begging
an opening
auditorium
once
within her grasp full
of promise and grace
get away come closer and
the constant waves the
waves
that keep her honest the
real jade
all that is.
She Must
Return
She cannot be lamb.

When all within
says fly girl fucking
fly
or swim
or risk being eaten alive on earth
dive and keep going honey forever
she stays only to go
though
yet again
beyond skin.

# ~Lullaby~

The stars lovely
tonight And the
moon
Nothing takes place of a
warm body
Heightened awareness
Observing feelings
Acknowledging loss Feeling
shock
And grace
And the love
of somebody
Another
You have not yet met
Your brothers' keeper
Lovers dreamer  Black
crow, large Encircling
rubbish
Vultures unaware of such
Kid on the balcony Coffee
gone cold

No music playing When
the band folds When

doves cry
And the humming of gaii Your
lullaby
Your go to
Your go to
In a desensitised world Can
you hear...

## ~ Light's ~

Standing at the traffic lights His fingers
sliding down my waist
Under my top Giving
me prickles His mouth
on mine I drink him
Completely
With a grin Whisk
and flutter Our
Lives are
changed
Forever...

# ~Jordan~

She moves me Her clear
cadence Love for the
occult And all things
vibed
He moves me His
struggle for love And
understanding
His need
For ripping off a bandages Her
need to be one
It's nice to be seen they said
Individually
Sphenoid's dancing
Sacrum's humming
And rhythm in time with the
wind Ocean
And
Moon
" you complete me "

## ~Name~

I am moved by sound of silence
ocean tides, stars
they ponder
I wander dark and night
As
society nor family define me
Those Saturday nights alone In a
world that breaks
my hands place knowingly Around
your waist
my prayers, not just for me But
for you too
Oceans Stars
Rivers
And moon drops She
Cries Your
name

# ~That~

Nothing
Nothing can ever get you like
that Like the power of two
Becoming one
When you feel like you are with your
magic self Other half
Dissolving the obsolete
Healing with kindness The
tragedies of this world
Unspokens

# ~Tattoo~

A gift
A dream
A pain
And nothing comes to you
While
You are running
Raindrops pendulums
Lighthouse in the dark The
house sits awake

Yet you
like to camp
in rivers And
oceans
In winds least likely
to provide comfort
And then you
Beautiful you
Tattooed In
My Mind....

# ~Snap~

Snap her up in a butterfly net
send her off to a Coconut Island
And he can't stop
Touching her And she
can't stop
Kissing him
As
This time....

# ~In~

They went in and out
Of each other's minds
Without any effort

# ~White~

How deep is your love?
It is October again land
of the Librans
Fliers dreamers believers
Sages forests and oceans
it was 1988
I still believed in love
And immortality my
brother left
while I dealt with bitter liaisons by so
called unconditionals Grasping
to whatever functional threads
kept them worldy
I chose to leave my body Subliminal
survival mechanisms
Sometimes
devoid of the heartbeat I was born with
I drank the sea, saw a hippy doctor
white cotton dress
unflattering to post-menopausal
bulges her red lippy
missing her lips
I wonder if she knows
I smile inside, whispering my holy fucks as

she issues Valium
like liquorice in a candy store I
wonder if she gets it
or at some point it
all got too hard
as she was struck off the board for
providing opiates
to lost souls in the tropics she
smiled
and meant it
Another tripper
in the land of maybes just
a story
Another fucking story
no wonder her lipstick misses love
And
another day in paradise…

# ~ Fine ~

Spirituality is not smoking a doobie
Or practicing Reiki
under a blue moon
feathers in your hair
hearts open,
attuned belief systems
Knowing a force outside
yourself Exists within
yourself
We think we have time So
we cruise
Or we think we have no time So
we rush
Missing it all
Oblivious to the beauty sitting in our vision
Are you o.k
just a verse A
question
Do you mean it
Eternally
Really
Truly?

It was 1973 Year
of the ox
Something about Vietnam I
don't remember it
I remember before
and after though
Isn't it ironic Alanis
Morisette pounds
the stage For that
moment,
I become her
And all that she is
Yum, I am ecstatic To
be born pure
Growing up on green earth
dirt and hills
fresh air of belonging
No
Cascaded with conditioning
Beyond our control
Initiating a madness

It was 1999
I sat on the couch with my papa
Talking dreams and fears Like
high school sweethearts His
tanned wrinkled hands
baggy pants
Blue eyes
grin and suntanned scalp How

I remember touching it Like
yesterday
Feeling timeless loves
circling his existence He
loved like no other
that man
And apart from my dog
I ache for his protective presence

It was 1993
My uncle dies of pancreatic cancer
Three months battling
A whirlwind Family
turbulence
Mum breaks her wrist, has it plated
Tarnished with grief beginning of storms
yet to happen

I am somehow cruising
My best year sporting wise and
personally Like I thrive
on punishment from the gods
To kick my arse
to channel it into something
Of value
A warped way to do things Yet
achievement
is false
A cover up for hurt
lack of understanding and control

You see
you think you are in charge In
control
Really, you are losing all control
Others admire you
for your determination To
get on
Yet the real ones Notice
the crumbling Inside
The grasping
at whatever holds us
you From tipping
Over That
Edge Like
egos
Battles for lashes
Strangers in the night You
can't sleep
Being good enough
Anchored
under study books, gym
memberships and veins

It was 1999
I get my first job offer And I
am in love Completely
With my boss The
practice The all
The moment danced
With horned angels

Horizons found

My newfound love Of
feeling
Energy through touch What a
ride
Katie makes the Olympics Wins a
gold medal
we both touch
I was there, dreamt it all earlier With
a little help
From my friends

It was 2000
I go see the fifteenth Rinpoche his
eminence
Tibetan horns and chanting,
Incense
It does things To
my cells
I feel blessed
I am in a container Falling
through the vortex There are
galaxies in my brain
Stars as my guide
colours flashing, parietals releasing,
legs shaking
memories
get erased from my soul Again
I am 23

I feel I am falling Help, I've
done it again They tell me I
may die
I didn't flinch
Must have known id be okay
Needed an excuse for a timeout
Anyway
He gets the call
His wife is dead, lying beside her baby She
had a stroke,
aneurysm or something Paints
a tragedy
Oh for fuck sake, Tom
My dear, dear bipolar friend Tom surely
he'd be cursing the gods, by now It's
always fucking something
His mother bellows, much like Jeannie Little

But with more grace Oh
for fuck sake
Why, why always the good ones?
I could not
Agree More
We all suffer Mark tells me Anna,
we all suffer you know
One breath at a time
He is gentle, thin and light
So delicate
He may disappear off a Tibetan mountain
He whispers stories

So calm
your skin breathes
He is ginger, borders on enlightenment Even
his dog
Looks like him I
love him
He teaches me so much I
break up with Matt It's a
familiar pain
Bordering on gut wrenching To
occasional relief and freedom

Hedonic pain
I must have deserved it,
bad wolf whispers Never
Never take relationships
personally He said
There is some relief In
that
We do though, hey?
Construct a story
Blame them, or ourselves
Our life
A mush of emotions and
relationships Babylon
It is a blue moon again
She whispers your name
The vision
Was for a room, a bed, some space Some
fucking respite

The drive has been so long And
on she goes
I say nothing

Have you noticed?
Nature bestows beauty
Kind, light, ever present
Walk gently
Humbly Be
careful
You're saying things The
threads
Are So
fine....

# ~ Faith ~

And in that moment
Love was lost
For with unsaids
So much more
Is available

The Aquarian mind
A little like mine
the blue moon
Complex and deep
Ethereal and real
Airhead yet grounded
Minuscule of madness
Random and astute
They get stuff
Know stuff They rarely
share It's like tentacles
Synapses in beauty
through artistic expression
Their truth conveyed
Welcome
To the age of
Aquarius

# ~Daniel~

He breathes her.
Always watching.
Oblivious to the noise.
Or her catching's,
and silent melodies echoing in her head.
He wants her oh, he
wants her
but he may have to share her. he
knows this.
For she is a bird and cannot be contained
in this realm, without shackles or some kind
of beheading at least She.
Wants him to drink her entirely.
Dive into her flesh leaving DNA
membranous footprints and love.
Inside her hips and
lips.
Every crevice.
Immeasurable in her veins
gaping at her neck
she knows he is to die for it
kills her softly.
She knows how to play Russian
roulette and she.

Regrettably,
is probably his greatest downfall
but there is a blindness
pulling an Applegate.
a web,
a string quartet sitting beside
them and if they should kiss,
the shackles fall down, the stars convulse and
the moon even gets trembly.
It is love gone wrong it is all
that it is not.
It is ancient and raw and ugly and beautiful
Perverse and serene yet calm and tranquil
a repeat of history.
but fuck. where
else,
other than the ocean can you
find a love like that?

# ~Rain~

She's always brilliant in the morning
her empty thoughts and
soft gaze forwards
he's always brilliant after coffee, a
shower and halfshave,
still dripping don't expect
her to stay,
she has been here before
is crimson like the wind,
sharper than your razor
And so much softer than your mum she
is the breeze before a storm crystal jade
in your ocean
and your heart
when it is torn
it is no oil painting until The
colours come to life and they
do
everyday in a
new way
only when she lets go of reason
And fortitude
And fucking depth of belonging the
colours are real

the earth is crying her name she
is only happy when it rains
this earth
she is only happy when it rains

# ~Dream~

Drunk and high and exposed to life
After all
We better get moving
There isn't much time
Your likeness to the sun and
the moon Where is your
heartbeat
Gazing into starlight eyes
Shocked and forgotten
Or Gazing soft eyes Warm
like tunnels Touching
Trying to make sense
Of
Nothing
Anymore

# ~God~

God enters the place
Of excess
Or defeat
Transparent
Or heavy
God enters the place
When there is nothing
Left
To ponder

# ~ Humanity ~

There's this song
called 'Anna Begins' by the Counting
Crows and I swear it's about me.
I stand at the front door like a
ghost
into a fog where nobody
notices
the contrast
of white on white.
Through the door I hear her crying.
I always hear her crying,
She said she'd like to meet a
boy who looks like Jesus.
She has trouble acting
normal when she's nervous.
I am not always like that, though.
Yet an edge to something can bring
out the colour in me.
I spend way too much time alone, and
can write of memories fallen, without
an ounce of understanding.
From You.

After all,
maybe it is better that way.
After recent raids, loss of innocent children,
personal relationships askew,
my soul could not, cannot
take much more.
Media will drop away in my world.
Again.
I may write fiction, I may not.
I sit with my papa the living dead.
At times he is present.
I am sure they're even baffled right now;
The spirits.
A man strums his guitar and sings rawly
of angels riding with us.
I like him already.
Wishing I was on the beach,
with him.
I think of Andrew and Harry
and wonder
if they know how much they mean.
I am dancing wildly to Sarah
McLaughlin's 'silence'
in my little city room lounge,
trancelike, a lava lamp melting.
He watches me
" You are beautiful just like that. You
have 'that thing' too you know."
hmm... I consider this and continue
to dance Alone.

And then over him Him,
red t shirt, balding, blue eyes,
long fingers.
Gets 'it'.
It.
Yet his melancholy and sensitivity send
blokes, scuttering for miles.
Her, I, me, I stick around.
Love is like that.
" Kiss me like you mean it " he pines.
It is difficult sometimes. They
echo one another,
and there is this push, pull, fly, run, melt,
hide, push, pull...going on,
when washed clean it surely should flow.
Shouldn't it?
She rescues him right back.
Old man above, a merlin, beggar,
wise soul... palms open,
" life, it is like polar opposites.
a series of pulls back and forth." he says
"which side wins?"
she asks, "love.
Love always wins..." ~ remember,
we bleed the same blood.

I wanna make love on a train,
cross-country
I wanna climb through your window
At three am
With the stars, shooting Just to
kiss your chest And hear you,
Whisper
my name...

# ~Tangent~

Like battles for lashes
crow's-feet for tapestries is
it any wonder
we broke down?
Blue eyed girls and
surfing mascots
begging to meet
in shimmery moonlight.
Yet people are afraid to admit
they don't understand.
That flaws are
a blemish or
worse,
a weakness.
Did you bear witness
when
you could have stepped in?
He stood over her said his
fearful goodbye
and left for work. A
third eye kiss
a touch for granted.
She had her last meal
Pawpaw, dried

then drove like a maniac
to the hills.
Through the hills
This was it This is
how
it had to happen. Vigils
were held prayers met
and messages sent
Unattainable. nobody
knows, but her.
Details are excruciating
messy and vile What
happened
was beyond measure
" look " she heard them say
" Another millimetre... and... " he
was glad to hold her again
hear her breathing under his arm Muffled
but tangible
Light. he
watches
her
asleep.
Her long hair brushes against his
shoulder
her light legs wrap around
his waist
her fingers stroke his jawline. Yet
all the love in the world and
in

his heart.
Could not
piece
the
puzzle
of what Had now become forevers
undone...

# ~ Full Moon Dreaming ~

So, she was full and intense this moon
shining bright on a still silent night balmy,
warm, stars were shining, southern cross,
Orion's scorpion
and bright Venus or Neptune,
I am never quite sure
the wolves were out in plenty
emotions and adrenaline running
high fine white lines dangerous
they can be bang!
Fright!
and some do not even know the
she wolf inside
there is yelling and noise,
The young drunk African boys out of control
Sitting on the bridge
four cop cars and noise
I am not sure anything is actually happening
I am just angry at ignorance and alcohol
and the unnecessary fuel it can create it
really burns with me that one
not sure why
I am not afraid though unafraid
really

only fear is my own
but there was calmness from the ocean my
favourite sound
I am praying by
my car alone
just praying  bike
man arrives I am
reminded
I love to ride my bike rather than drive a
hint of envy envelopes me
I want that freedom again I
like that Anna
he sits and then approaches "got any
weed?" he innocently asks
"umm, no. Sorry"
never sure why I apologise for this
"I don't smoke it" we
get chatting
wow, he has a sore back, lower spine from
years of cycling
I treat him on the grass under
the full moon
tune into his craniosacral rhythm and
feel his energy
oh my goodness,
what a beautiful soul this man has is
I physically realign,
right sacral torsion, tight glutes, stretching then,
the eyes
I have been challenged with brown eyes

of late and my judgement has dissolved
his eyes.
I travelled straight through inside of him I
have barely ever had that experience
or maybe he went through me no,
I went in them
wow
it was so lovely a
travelling
instant calmness  a
want for nothing a
noncraving
he is brother
this is is so beautiful brown and
deep and inviting I asked for
nothing remember
I was sitting praying quietly by my car he
camps, makes soapstone necklaces,
had a beard and gap in his teeth, a dimple but
eyes that went forever
there was no instant attraction initially I
thought he may be a bit goofy
on spending time
he looked more like Woody Harrelson
I have a soft spot for him and his gapped teeth but
where he is and what he gets
can never be expressed or shown here ever
we travelled together
he has a child and has been
exploring consciousness,

had his shit but so open to loving still
has his shit but open to loving
a landscape gardener that was requiring and
desiring connection
maybe intimacy
aren't we all in that moon language
desiring connection that is...? and
maybe human ness
he opened my mind to knowing good
ones exist
yes!
I saw him more than his mates apparently
we did yoga and the rest was a dream the
internal battle persists
persisted
the rest was a dream
so I am going to tell you the dream we
go to the water
with a towel full
starlit night
warm with a moon that was
so felt so felt
so felt touching
progressed
could this be happening ... really?
Is this irresponsible? Damaging? Bad? She
has morals this she wolf that has lived By
maintaining desires and being good
or maybe this was not living
plus she knows herself

the bit that always wants more and
the bit of only making love with
one you love
holy crap something was going
on here something beyond
ordinary
and in this time it did not really matter
nothing really mattered
she finally gave in and listened to
her body that is okay
that is okay
in fact that is fucking wonderful naked with
Jesus under the shining moon
oh please hold that image
strikingly fucking amazing
making play love on the sand on a towel,
stroking a masculine jaw and dimple
stroking an unloved face
strong jawline and heart
that has been battered and bruised
kissing an unshaven chest  drawing on
an unshaven chest stroking biceps
embracing masculine
he loves her breasts the
shape
and her hips but
the breasts
and feeling a heart beat fast inside
a barrel chest
and she is treated gently and

lovingly
and gently what
is real?
Then the monkey unleashes and
she is ok with that becoming
animalistic
and expansive she
never does this
and both act on passion just
feeling in the moment no
agendas
he picks her up she is
straddling him
and there is nothingness just
some noise something
the ocean
them
wolves in the night
the she wolf she has been fighting exists
and is living
fucking living in this strangest of fire lit nights no
inhibitions
apart from the stray wandering
the beach alone in search of
something no
judgement
she felt protected and remotely calm only
slight fear at what was happening then the
wild woman went "fuck it" the secret smile
inside

"you have always wanted to
be this do this
be uninhibited and reckless and free so ....
Be it be ok
"let your mind go"
beyond the caressing and touching and veils
visualise the feelings
the feelings with us
desires and harmless loving and
unrequited fire
it was pure fire she felt
"you look like someone she says"
"Jesus" he replied
"I have been told"
naked under a full moon with Jesus laughter
at the insanity of it all
they burst out into laughter it is funny
it is totally weird and crazy
crazy beautiful but ok
he was not like others oh
my oh lordy my
her mother would have a hernia and if she
(I) heard it from someone else
she would think it was totally cool
her Alanis moment arrival
the jewel in the night never ever
been done before
in her experience she would
have stopped, given in to
responsibility

oh what a full moon moment she
cannot blame the moon though
it was not that
it does not even matter what is was but
it happened a moment in time where it
stood still and both parties were present
and got one another
can it get any better than that?
maybe
what if it can
and we all acted on loving not
sexual loving
but the entering of soul travel
through loving imagine
imagine
and stretch into the vastness Of
what is out there
this is a dream remember
it is just a dream
and sometimes we are in this body. love
up SHE WOLVES!!

# ~Bardot~

There's this thing in floating
Drifting with nothing to do She's
learning the hard way She's
learning the loud way She's
learning the only way To make
you her lover
call you another And draw
out your blue
Her hidden smiles and quiet Bardot's
The ultimate love The
dance of
She keeps
No
secrets
from
You...

It's a depend on nothing fast blowing breeze
We wear our betrayals unguarded
Our purchases in our stomachs
An overflowing of everything and
nothing
Until we realise we have
We are
Nothing
It's an aching to be light free When
humans are futile Compared with
the earth at play It's
a fast rush
A hanging on to her Labrador And
leaning over to smell her again
As she loves you As no
one else should
but does
Regardless
It's a race against time When
time seems the winner
And then you stop

Breathe in the stars And
remember who you are

And why it is
That you Love
The smell Of
Dogs...

# ~Mess~

A beautiful mess
You dance inside of me
He sits
Hands clawed
Nails driven
Heart beating
She drives
Eyes clear
Hair wild
Hands waiting
The world
Has gone mad
He said
We aren't It is
Winds blow
Capes fall Oceans
roar Then
the child spoke In
colour
And the clouds woke

An echo Of
afterlives
You My love

Anna Grace

Are such
A
beautiful
mess.

# ~Delusions~

She stands in the wind But
never waves bye bye She
doesn't believe
In modern love
Or any orchestrated ideal
Of how it's meant to be
She's not hard
Nor a man hater Quite
the opposite Actually
Soft as mush Falling
to the calls Real
Don't fall for me
He said
Looking into her eyes
Guiding her waist Hands
on her breasts Deliberate
She strokes his face His
beard
His broken eyes
And that jaw Alive
So much potential
I won't
She assured him
I won't

She broke her rules
It was a fuck
On the couch In
the shed
She broke her rules But
needed to feel Regain a
moment Familiarise
He has
So much potential
And she
Howls with the moon
Breaks with the sun
Bends on the sand And
loves to hold Another
Yet a demon Sits
waiting
Delusional
Relationships
They're fucked I
am more
So much More
than that
Be careful Coz
you Are
Too...

# ~Tear Drops~

He sits on her bed Palm
in hands Crumpled in ash
Like a lonely old man
Or little boy forgotten Broken
He could get like that
He looked cute when he cries though She
doesn't quite know what to do with it
Why does she always wear the pants?
It's my heart he says, my heart
I give you everything and I just...
Don't do this, she says Don't....
You choose
To give yourself away like that I tell
you not to give everything Coz then
you are left
Always wanting more Empty
And I cannot,
cannot give that to you, she says
They were fire and air
Hansel and Gretel Cupid
and rose
Black and white
and many
Many shades of beautiful

It was always going to happen He saw
her with kids on their hike And spoke
of her being a great mum You don't say
that to a number five
She'll run a mile Even
if it were true She
softens
Sits behind him Hugs
him,
kisses his whiskers
and places his slender fingers inside
her mouth A tear trickles and
smile beckons
She touches his dimple
And apologises Meaning it
Promising to be more conscious
Of her sharp words
And wicked ways
Gentle souls, both of them
They did this
Like a series of polar opposites Pulling
Him up her down
Her down Him up
Sometimes
they flat lined
to bliss Heavens
gates
away from pressure
Which side wins?
Love wins Love

always wins
Doesn't it?
Although In
this case
nothing did...
To miss moments And an
always presence
They
Are
Welcome
Again...

# ~Sydney strangers~

It was 1996, a trip to Sydney and
stay with my brother.
A break from chemotherapy and a
life of unruly routine ravaging my
young body
I had red boxers on, white
tank top as I sat in the
big double bed watching
movies, freaking myself
out, home alone
with Brad Pitts seven.
Fitting.
What a strange movie, emotive
raw and sick our human condition.
I'd pray, and wonder and
wish to feel better, normal
again.
I felt embarrassed,
had to exit Uni, and my hockey
comeback.
Practical realities.
Yet was 'told'
I may die without chemo. Pfft
I'd never do it now.

Dirty magazines and sports manuals lined
the spare room
overlooking the harbour. It
was a long way down.
I would gaze out the doors.
Bereft of shadows.
Wind through curtains.
But I always felt good in my brother's bed,
like wearing a lover's jumper in winter.
I drifted in and out of healing
Frustration to surrender.
It was fucked, really.
Andrew had a flash apartment with
a pool on the roof, or ground I can't
remember.
He lived in many places.
Palaces and dives Many
things
I don't know the whys of.
He was playing businessman
and pretty wrapped up
In his own self-importance.
Yet to me he was.
I detected an edge of cockiness I
did not approve of.
And greed.
That wasn't my brother.
Later traced to an exuberant boss. I
get wary of those who get too big for
their boots, too quickly.

Anywhere.
It was a backyard business ran
from the apartment
associated with the UK, his previous home.
He was going to be a millionaire.
Apparently.
Again, cocky
Yet I was just grateful To be
alive at this point Wishing
many things.
My health and return for Uni. My
dream to be a physiotherapist
His secretary was the barmaid he won
over up from the local pub.
She was pretty, long hair,
slender and a local.
He had a knack for that.
Comes with divine looks cheeky smile
and naive belonging.
He just couldn't help it.
They fell at his feet, those
lotus leaves.
Rarely did he have to fight for it.
Yet, inherently he was kind.
They later married and made babies.
They fitted well, still do, and
rely upon one another.
Life partners.
So maybe there is something in
destiny.

Or history. Or
biography.
She took me to the cross,
I'd never been before.
She was a Sydney girl through and through.
I was a child of the universe. It
was seedy, dirty and made of
dreams of the underworld.
There were prostitutes,
trannies and young boys, about eleven
waiting to be picked up
by wealthy businessmen, suited in flash cars My
stomach churned in despair.
I can still see their startled faces, and
the eyes of men
who knew they were doing wrong I
wasn't nearly as innocent
as she predicted though. She
didn't know me at all.
I was neutral.
Secretly my body knew
I would conquer this illness and
discover many gifts, later. I would
have died otherwise.
I saw stuff I didn't share.
For premonitions I didn't know.
And saw through bullshit and chivalry.
Even my own.
There was a class thing, Our
souls didn't take easily,

It was more of a forced belonging.
They can suck.
Require maintenance.
Exhausting realities. Never
ease continuums.
Andrew confessed
She had a boyfriend already.
He tended to do that. Not
sure what he wanted me to
do about it.
Yet I loved
when he came clean with me.
They lived a bit of a fantasy, fast
cars, drinking, pools
and promise of moneys.
Lots.
He tended to rescue the doves
getting treated badly.
Some kind of unresolved
mother wound I suspect.
They bathed and baked by the pool.
Masquerades.
Good-looking young couple
planning an exotic lifetime I'll
admit I wanted her body.
She was sleek with long legs,
and attractive face.
And I prayed id get the strength to
get my athleticism
And self back. It was

a shit time;
cortisone and steroids
do horrid things to one physically.
Drain the system. People
worried.
Thought they had to protect me. I
was sick had to rest and heal.
I wasn't really.
I was being challenged To
face unvoiced demons and
sacred stab wounds.
I was out of my body
more than I was in.
I see that now.
Family grounds me with a thud, Not
always so graceful.
You think I'd learn.
People are afraid of illness, Especially
unvoiced, transparent and not so
ugly in your face.
You could think I was faking it,
yet I swear
I know what to be ' nearly dead '
feels like.
More than most.
I don't recommend it
Either.
Yet greater warriors have faces bigger
burdens In rougher terrains.
I still had familial relationship and

loyalty during this time. Maybe it
was an expectation, what you do.
Back then.
Yet,
there is something ever
so beautiful about caring
for those you love deeply.
Really.
Surely, it should heal you too.
If you let her.
A privilege reserved For the
gods and sages.
A bare witnessing
A soul unravaged
Rebirths in taking.
Despite soul contracts This
helped my healing.
And I am lucky.
Yet there is a stark realisation
Maybe I haven't grown up yet.
It's true.
And those forever there's are
not really there.
And it becomes a selfish world
I do not understand.
For fires ' just ' kept burning Even
though I was
And always Will
Be Free To Fly
Thank you

# ~All~

In embracing the madness you
must ask
do I love all of you in all
of me
all the closets
hidden enigmas
all the dresses and
changing bra cups
ridges and wrinkles
sagging and dimples and
does he
who walks in all his glory with
his masculine jaw dimple and
growth
bare chest
sexed up
surely this
is the penultimate
mountain
the fountain of
youth
a time of
the 60s' Woodstock
child renewal

of dancing beards and
fearless dresses far too
short
for any pearly
imagination
to dance
into stranger worlds of
echoing embers ashes
and firelight clouds
so life goes on she
just does
the waves will crash in the
moon will shine
a star will drop regardless
of your mountains your
aching
your seething and dreaming
the cavernous holes
begging and bleeding in
all the crevices
at the table you
thought
you no longer owned not
all the pretty ones though
they make her
smile
in her sleep so
step up and
embrace your
madness it is all

ok seemingly
in the end
rise
with the tiding changes and
don't submit
fully
ever
until he knows until
he shows he
can
surely
love all
of you....

# ~Breathe~

I never heard dad once say ' I love you '
maybe I have
But it was like a forced reaction Some
kind of choking mechanism
Forged against his Capricornian brain He
didn't mean to
He lived in a black bubble oblivious
to the noise
Of anyone else's cravings
Mum would whisper it
Through gentle actions or in
times of need
And in her way
Or only say it on the phone a
kind of distant
telepathic integration I love saying I love you it's real
KA and I would always say love you girl And
she'd embrace me
like the entire universe, itself
Breathe my embers
and fucking mean it
' I Love you ' is not light though It matters
It took me ages to say it to Matt but
when we whispered

the ' I ' word After a night
of chaos
under covers Our
beings changed
and merged
forever
I loved saying that I
love you
And feeling that I
love you
I love you I
love you I
do.......

# ~Cave~

Bodies
Entangled
Caves
In The
Snow

# ~ Cars ~

In writing truth one may shudder
Yet it is the truth
It was 1999; I was in a good space,
and final year at uni after many mishaps including
illness that almost cost me my degree.
A dear boy had been chasing me, I had resisted,
we were sapiosexual and he caught me,
or maybe, finally, I,
Him finally, I Him..
My love of his brain, his mind, turned
him sexy, for me.
We just fit.
After I pushed him relentlessly for fear
of him seeing my dark side.
He could be goofy and annoying, slightly
feminine in nature and I was sure I wanted a 'man'.
We were together for ages before any intimacy
were friends and our first erotic experience
was fully clothed, in my lounge room, with
my friend asleep on the couch.
It was amazing.
Amazing.
I had a pink low cut top and black Levis.
He had these long fingers, gentle and divine,

the insides of me were rocking.
I could barely breathe, it was excruciatingly yummy,
and we broke our friendship thingy,
there was no going back.

He did already know the lower and higher
parts of me and I didn't give him nearly enough credit.
Who was I kidding, he was already highly
evolved and I was just coming into my own.
We would kiss the night before I had a work
trip—that was my way to avoid commitment,
kiss and then run.
He lived next door for god sake, and his mother
loved me.
One night his car was stolen.
A second hand black Saab his pride and joy
I heard something at 2 am but thought nothing
of it I had never seen him so pissed off,
he strode the street
swearing, close to tears.
I felt helpless.
The cops called and said it had been found
and trashed in the hills.
So that was good news.
We made love for the first time, that night.
I will say love coz it wasn't sex. It had
been six months in waiting.
To me this was a sacred act that had to be earned.
This entry to my being, my yoni, my soul
I loved myself enough to view this pleasure

as that. He had done his time, and I know
it drove him crazy.
The build-up was lovely, kissing thighs and
tickling the lower parts of me he did
so well, like no other.
It took me places, to the river and oceans. I
embraced it and fortunately he loved it.
He was so happy, we were meant to be rescuing
his car. Parts were not comfortable yet
I knew him well enough to ask and change things.
I loved kissing his chest and letting my hair
fall down to his navel.
Penetration was good. It cemented our
standing our relationship.
There was no dominance just mutual understanding,
love and laughs.
We had done it, deepened us, he had
me now, and off we went hooning through
the hills in rescue of
his car, which had been trashed,
yet no longer mattered in the scheme of things,
we'd just committed our sacred act kali,
Kundalini, rising,
and an extra step in 'us'.
Nothing else matters when
love is around
and you feel protected and held.
Completely. I
believe, no, I
know

my work, led me to this point,
I had been unravelling enough, to be there.
The fun, laughs.
Beginning and ending.
I love him. I
loved this. I
love this...
Anna Hookings

# ~You~

She strode corridors
Of
lonely ghosts
Dolls
of the underground
Angels
in waiting.
Emergence of light
She
danced the
edges
Of times
And beginnings.
Queried death
Then
life
Finding There
may
be neither.
Let
your gift
Be

Compassion
And your
Presence.

# ~Thee~

There Is no god
When you Free-
fall Into space
In heavens
Surreal
There is no god
When you Are
shunned
By a lover Yet
embraced
By another You
don't Even want
There's no god
Until
You are bare
Naked Blood
falling Deranged
Risking it all For
another
Your integrity And
body Intact
Your name
Nameless
Form

Formless
A guise
There is no god Until
The only
Choice left Is
To fly
Be the witness
Witnessing In
loving
In loving
Entirely In
Loving Thee

# ~Memory~

Unfortunately, Or
fortunately
I tend to remember pretty
much everything.
Photos on the tractor with my brother at eighteen
months, the photographer blowing bubbles to
get my attention, my cruddy stockings way too large
it gave me a huge crutch, Andrew being silent,
for pretty much five years as Kimbo the Labrador
played vigil at his bedside. Dad would smoke peter
Jackson cigarettes and take off around the farm,
and for a moment,
or many, he was my outlaw hero.
He was also good-looking in a rugged farmly way.
And I'm a little scared I
have his eyes.
Piercing blue.
Mum was the perfect maiden, far
from token wife,
her ritual of shower and makeup and
cooking for shearers,
all of whom loved her, and
her cooking,
and probably secretly wanted to

get into her pants.
Her beauty was, and is
rare,
and even more stunning when
one is oblivious to it.
Yet, her boundaries were huge,
there were snippets reserved for children
and rare friends, and maybe even her husband
in times gone by.
Yet, she would never show it.
Like crying or emotion were weaknesses.
You just never did it.
Andrew and I would go to her in our tender
moments, a beacon of light, mother Teresa,
princess Diana of sorts.
Her daddy adored her, her
mother
depended on her
She was afraid of me and my 'wild' - never got it,
yet never seemed to want to either.
Andrew was sookier than me, I had this
kind if farm girl resistance which held me in
good stead with the natives.
I was liked, salt of the earth and sporty.
When my nan died I felt her presence in
the lounge, she was slightly neurotic and controlling.
A strange disjointed energy.
Rushed, busy, buzzing.
Control.
Such s blasphemy I would later learn.

I don't know who held it the most.
Mum gave in to keep peace.
Dad fought with unknown entities.
I watched on. There
were rules, we were
kids, but generally
we were pretty free.
I tend to remember pretty much everything,
my brother became my hero
For some peculiar reason I needed heroes in
my life. He was my mate until male friends
came over then he'd be too cool for me and
go all gangster.
Not gentle, how he was when it
was just the two of us.
I resented this.
I was sensitive, some things never change
I still ache for loyalty and persistence though,
and the laying of truth on the table, no matter
how hurtful or unbearable it may seem.

Kids, they break too,
or at least adapt and develop their own
strategies for coping.
I never saw dad cry, only get sad, dishevelled
or angry, often.
I saw mum cry, once,
maybe twice,
once on the floor in her bedroom,
over me.

I was devastated.
It was enough to break me,
and then change me.
It showed me it really fucking mattered.
She didn't even cry when her own mother
passed. In public anyway
I am sure I am the emotional vessel set to
express what my family can't or couldn't.
I had to accept unsaids.
Unsaids are so much more potent and
hurtful than saids They cause cancers
and frailty and tragedies, beyond
reasonable measure.
Papa was my angel.
Still is.

Animals are my saviour.
Many farming families have strange
upbringings, perhaps with good intentions,
go greedy or lack perhaps a vision they
had for themselves.
Everyone has their dreams,
everyone has their place.
Love is a fate.
Love is a birthright.
A given. A
necessity.
A plight.
A living, in light, moment by moment

If you have little ones
encourage their wildness,
Hold them tight,
Give them rules with
abandonees faith
and encourage them to roam free.
Free.
Hold those you love most Close...
And. never ever... .walk away...

# ~Katie~

It was 97 or 98, she had come round to see me, I was a little battle worn having chemo for a disease I didn't have, nor want. Katie was happy, in the Australian squad, living at the AIS. We had made our state debut together, junior and senior, travelled through shit and joy. But, this was her moment, of truth. Her coming out, to tell me she was gay, and in love with shell, another team member. I was happy for her, no hint of sexual jealousy, except maybe at her newfound freedom and lifestyle, Pisceans' are romantic dreamers, and this was taking huge courage. As if I didn't already know, though.
I worried, as she'd fall hard and I didn't want her to see her get hurt. Later, ultimately, she did, but this was her debut, her first, love. It was real. Our friendship was so deep and profound such boundaries were never crossed. Potent unspokens and understanding. We loved one another, period. Mum was spun put, yet accepted it. I got a teddy to take to chemo, and KA being who she is wanted to join me. Who would want to do that? In we went, I sit in the big chair, puffy and refrained for dying people around me. It was a sterile, putrid environment; I always felt I was back in the sixties. Nurses were extra bubbly bursting out if their skin as if making up for the mortality surrounding them. They always had trouble getting a vein, I'd become used to it by now. Not the material going in, though, each time was

different; I could feel it traverse my blood vessels, a poison entering my membranes. Katie squirms, and somehow sees me as brave. I, see her as brave. What kind if mate gives up training to watch someone have poison injected into their system? Fuck, it takes a special person to say fuck it, fall in love, declare it, own it, be it and live it. Like she does, even now. If coming out is to be her only moment, she does, it with style, and grace.God. Katie Allen,
I love you so.

# ~Nineteen~

It was 1993, perhaps my best year to date.

Uni was busy and good, I made team of the year
that year, for the south Australian league in hockey,
I was grounded focused alive.
My mother's brother got diagnosed with pancreatic
cancer in the November, gone the following February.
That rocked boats, including mine.
Especially my grandparents, and mum fell off
a ladder and broke her wrist requiring plates
and surgery, storing bitter, grief-ridden emotions.
She'd heard Graham had been drinking
and partying heavily.
A Croser man trait Not my
mother's style to
step in and say anything though.
Seen as noble.
Part of me sees it as stupid. Family
rules and conditions.
I had been down in the morgue, science
lab preparing for exams.
Small intestines, guts, stomachs, the pancreas,

Prior to meeting my brother to go and see

Graham and Lou in the hospital.
Perhaps not the greatest timing I
am a feeler.
" There is nothing they can do " I
remember Lou saying.
Graham sat there like a big lost child.

Fuck, I thought, this is cruel.
This is big.
I spent a lot of time visiting Graham. And, the family. I was
right into family then.

When he died my brother came to my flat, with
his girlfriend.
And he held me tight.
That I remember. God, it
was good.
Andrew can never front emotions alone.
He'd usually have to bring someone, for courage.
At Graham's funeral, my papa asked me to stand
next to him and catch his tears.
I did it.
That just about broke me.

Lou looked beautiful holding a single rose as his
niece played that on her acoustic guitar.
And of course things got messy after that;
In a number of senses, drunken sibling rivalry, wills, loss of
a lover and maybe some truths, hard and tumbling. His last
Christmas, he was a stick with huge hands and legs blown up

with oedema.
He reminded me of an African.
These huge, huge hands and frail body
He'd wheel his chair back out to us, for another stout.
He was never going to miss out on a party.
Ever.
Probably still doesn't.
It was the year Madonna visited to Adelaide.
I'd go running through the city with secret hopes
of gaining a glimpse.
Seriously.
She was one of my hero's.
The concert was amazing.
It began with topless black women
sliding down poles.
She was clever sexy and serene.
I was short and had to stand on a chair.

It was an emotional night as one of my greatest friends got crazily drunk and hurled some abuse at me I did not see coming.
Jealousy and love over friendships.
She had my bed for the night and I slept on the floor in Rachel's room.

I can remember feeling exhausted, hurt, and seething.
It was only, because we cared deeply and
were running partners.
Friends meant everything to me. Cat
would so usually have my back.

Gosh life can be silly.

She later came into work to buy beer and ask me to the movies to make up for her drunken slur.
I actually took a bit to forgive.

Must have respected myself back then.
Model student studying physio and playing national league hockey
An inner faith.

I was in my body.
In my mind, although a busy life, things couldn't be much better.
I had a lot to learn
Delusional success.
And being ok when hearts were breaking around me Yet I was pretty resilient.
Men came and went yet I never searched.
Hamo would visit from the country.
Had a genuine thing for me, was goofy, sexy and warm.
Somehow we just never did make it through.
My aunty Gillie died that year, too.
She lost a leg, gangrenous, from smoking, and I remembered vividly her phantom limb pain.
And being intrigued by it
She had the heart of a soldier, and welcoming touch. She was widow of my papa's brother Stan.
I spent a lot of time with her too for some reason.
Meaningful relations.

I had a premonition dream she was going to die.
And she did. Two
weeks later.

During a state hockey tournament, Juliet took
me aside to tell me. I had a horrid time,
then went and played a blinder.
I tend to do that.
Need a tragedy to inspire me.
Like I'm doing it for them somehow.
Easier when for another
Poor mum, she lost a lot that year too.
Gosh, I am just seeing that now.
I don't give her nearly enough credit.
Her suffering is always so silent.
Her wrists stored the pain, as she worked
and worked, cooking, gardening, and caring
for others. She lost her brother.
I must remember that.
I don't know who I think I am sometimes.
Get wrapped up in my own self-importance.
Andrew mum papa and I stood at Grahams grave.
I have a great photo capturing that moment.
Of love's, unspokens.
Blood strength.
Grandma turned to God, Papa to carnations,
his garden, footy and Grandkids.

Grandma went extra churchy, I only realised after mum
mentioned it once, you know, the old ' a parent should never

have to bury their child first ' thing.
I get it.
She used to hang out washing with a cigarette
hanging from her mouth.
I think she felt she had been burnt.
She also hardened. I see it now. Yet she was still a
bosomly mother and token grandma in every sense.
I had three bikes stolen that year.
Got through it.
Sport and hockey and friends my greatest ally.
They got me through anything,
and sometimes I liked the secret struggle.
Insomnia began.
Probably due to burnout, adrenals and emotions.
I worked in pubs till 4 am, it was fun.
I flew with the wind Was
light as a feather And
gave a shit
About most things.....'
I was only nineteen.

# ~Pack~

Kids of narcissists
Grow up
With a bit of delusion
That control is normal
Belittling encouraging Cold
comforting
It will break you Turn
you hard Misled
Or rebellious
Or make you so transparent
The lost loving
Will move you In
ways
To inspire
Yourself And
The packs...

# ~*Time*~

Which way will you run When
it's always
All around you The
feeling Lost
And found you Again The
feeling
That we have no control
Keep asking ourselves Are
we strong enough?
From your heart
The branches grow deeper, For
what
Nobody knows There
is a world We've
never seen And in
darkness We reach
for love But
I'll reach for you Where time
never goes....
Anna

# ~Shacks~

But she can't,
because she doesn't know
herself Doubt
Something like hate has cut
through her world
Like a shack Shattering
enchantments
of secret nights...

# ~*Hurt*~

When the hurt
And the healer
collide

# ~Nothing~

It occurred to me today
it did
if I did nothing
And faded far far away
But just did nothing
the outcome would be the same
as
doing everything

## ~Boy~

He finishes
Her sentences

## ~ Him ~

A new moon in moon time
He'll come round she tells me
Pearls like greys
innocent beginnings like
all of us
she does not know this man
his vicious afterlives thorn
like behaviour
I pray so too
but know the muse in me dances
as Ii dive underwater
safety from the world as
he
he sits blue
eyed long
haired perfect
skin
and long fingers cultured
to holding her he who sits
waiting
for the dance of rivers
mountains moving a
saner world devoid of
machines

and harshlike conditioning his
dreadlocks shine
eyes turquoise to royal navy he
smiles your name
as you drink his heart And
the void of love you just
brushed
on his shoulders...

# ~Blue~

Boys posing as men
Fast cars
Sunset boulevards
Child smiles
Dog whispers
Moon beams
And I
Still
Miss you madly

# ~ *Fly* ~

She was four.
Hair tied back, holds a white kitten.
Pink dress. Bunch of posies. Other
girls wanted her hair.
Picture perfect, yet she
already sensed
things were amiss.
In the world.
Her mother liked The
girly stuff.
She.
Was already floating above it,
looking from a distance.
Yet desperately wanting
the embrace.
The cardinal one with
no conditions. You
know the one. where
the universe swallows
you whole
and you traverse the birth canal In a
good and noble way.

Like an atom exploding.
Love births.

Love bombs.
The kind felt when you and
your best mate
hang out drinking tequilas for
the first time.
And hug and love.
Love so deep like no other.
Conditional LOVE ... WHO
MADE THAT UP?
She was eight
When she flew out the window
Of a rolling car.
It was her birthday, slow
motion,
wet roads no seatbelt.
Worth a chapter.
Laughing, turned upside down.
She woke with blood everywhere.
Fractured collarbone. Alone in
the grass.
Raining.
Panic as they couldn't find her.

Outside herself again.
Her birthday in a hospital bed
with a sling.
She was nine.
Her father was pushing Up
against her mother at the
fridge.

Mum was saying "get out." He
was laughing.
She felt embarrassed And wanted
to punch her dad
For some reason..
Yet he was showing affection,
Wasn't he?
She never once saw them kiss.
Odd.
Oh maybe a goodbye. More
duty than pleasure Maybe
she was adopted.
After all.
There were screaming matches.
Mood swings,
Peter Jackson cigarettes, lies,
laughs, deceit and a life
of work on the land.
She had sport, animals, her brother
(sometimes )
and nature.
God, for a while. And
the sky to go to.
Now.
She is washing herself clean.

www.ingramcontent.com/pod-product-compliance
Lightning Source LLC
Chambersburg PA
CBHW020416080526
44584CB00014B/1353